This book belongs to

_____

_____

Includes 2 each of 25 Waterlily, Lotus, Ponds, and Watergarden coloring images by Selina Fenech.

As an artist, color is a thing of magic in my life. Color creates shapes, forms, and feelings in the artworks I paint. Laying color onto a blank page is when I feel closest to true magic, when I feel happiest and most relaxed, and it's through what I create that I share my love of magic with the world. Through my coloring books I want to share that same magic with you.

The designs in this book are not the usual fantasy images you may expect from my work. I grew up surrounded by ponds, lilies and wildlife, and this collection of realistic designs is my tribute to the beauty of watergardens.

When designing my books I decided to print them with two copies of each design, because as an artist I know there are always so many possibilities! I also wanted to give everybody the chance of a do-over with every design in case of an oops (as an artist I know that happens too!). Try a different medium, or a different colour scheme. Or share the magic with a friend, child, parent, or sibling. Because sharing your creativity and joy of color is the best magic of all.

See the colors the artist chose for her paintings at
www.selinafenech.com

Ponds and Flowers - Beautiful Watergardens Coloring Book
by Selina Fenech
First Published May 2017
Published by Fairies and Fantasy PTY LTD
ISBN: 978-0-6480269-3-8

Artworks Copyright © 2016 Selina Fenech. All rights reserved.
No part of this book may be reproduced in any form or by any electronic or mechanical means including information storage and retrieval systems, known now or hereafter invented, without permission in writing from the creator. The only exception is by a reviewer, who may share short excerpts in a review.

Using This Book

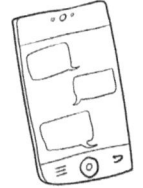

Turn off and move away from distractions. Relax into the peaceful process of coloring and enjoy the magic of these fantasy images.

Experiment! There is no right or wrong way to color, and with two of each image, there's no pressure.

This book works best with color pencils or markers. Wet mediums should be used sparingly. Slip a piece of card behind the image you're working on in case the markers bleed through.

Don't be scared to dismantle this book. Cut finished pages out to frame, or split the book in half where the second set of images start so you and a loved one can color together.

Never run out of fantasy coloring pages by signing up to Selina's newsletter. Get free downloadable pages and updates on new books at -
selinafenech.com/free-coloring-sampler/

Share Your Work

Share on Instagram with #colorselina
to be included in Selina's coloring gallery,
and visit the gallery for inspiration.

selinafenech.com/coloringgallery

Second Set of Pages Begins Here

When designing my books I decided to print them with two copies of each design, because as an artist I know there are always so many possibilities! I also wanted to give everybody the chance of a do-over with every design in case of an oops (as an artist I know that happens too!). Try a different medium, or a different colour scheme. Create without fear! Or share the magic with a loved one. Because sharing your creativity and joy of color is the best magic of all. ~ *Selina*

About the Artist

As a lover of all things fantasy, Selina has made a living as an artist since she was 23 years old selling her magical creations. Her works range from oil paintings to oracle decks, dolls to digital scrapbooking, plus Young Adult novels, jewelry, and coloring books.

Born in 1981 to Australian and Maltese parents, Selina lives in Australia with her husband, daughter, and growing urban farm menagerie.

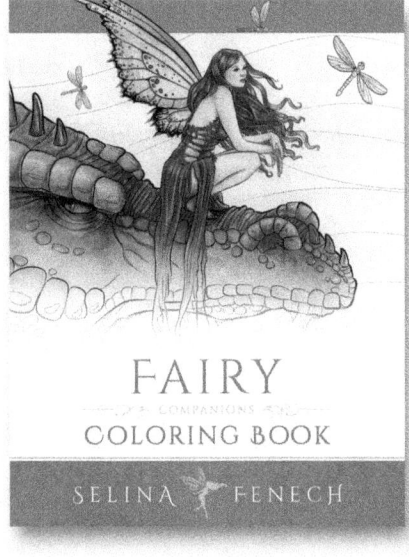

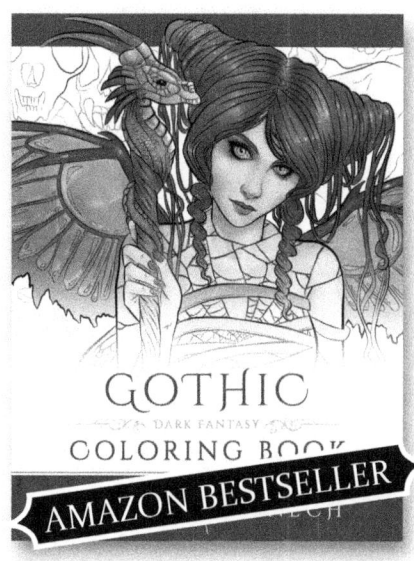

See all books online at viewauthor.at/sfcolor

Share Your Work

Selina loves to see your finished designs and the colors you chose!
Share online with #colorselina

www.facebook.com/selinafenechart
www.selinafenech.com

www.ingramcontent.com/pod-product-compliance
Lightning Source LLC
Chambersburg PA
CBHW060529010526
44110CB00052B/2547